Stephen Gray: SELECTED POEMS 1960–92

Stephen Gray

SELECTED POEMS 1960–92

DAVID PHILIP Cape Town Johannesburg

First published 1994 in Southern Africa by David Philip
Publishers (Pty) Ltd, 208 Werdmuller Centre, Newry Street,
Claremont, 7700 South Africa
© 1994 Stephen Gray

ISBN 086486 238 5

Printed and bound by Clyson Printers, 11th Avenue, Maitland,
7405 South Africa

CONTENTS

Introduction ix

The Discovery 1
Snake 1
Sunflower 2
Zebra 2
The Tame Horses of Vrededorp 3
Rounding the Cape 4
The Horny Crew 4
Fatter than they Knew 5
Cecil John 6
Beauty Tames the Beast 6
Specimen 7
It's about Time 8
Wolraad Woltemade 8
Siren 9
Eggs 10
Homecoming 10
Isandhlwana 11
Battlehill 11
Cataract 12
Quarry 12
Veldfire 13
Totems 13
A South African Christmas 14
Mayfair 16
Afar in the Desert 18
Hottentot Venus 19
Song of the Gold Coming In 20
Song of the Raiders 22
In Memoriam: Olive Schreiner 23
Fernando Pessoa 24
Divers, Reunion Island 25
Local History 26
Birth of a Seal 26
The Suicide 27
To a Young Poet 27
Poetry Reading 28
Mermaid 28
Mother and Son 29
Grand Parade, September 1976 29
Adamastor's New Year Bulletin, 1976-7 30
Thomas Bowler's Kalk Bay 31

My Father's Watercolour, 1918 32
Outriding 32
No Way 34
Letter to her Husband 34
Love Poem, Hate Poem 35
How Could You Forget? 35
Last Train 36
The Function of Poetry 36
Underwater Music 37
Correspondence 37
The Witness 38
Night Song 38
Assemblage 39
The Historical Moment 41
The Herb Garden 42
Incident at Pennington 42
Apollo Café 44
The Sun Room 46
Crossing the Desert 49
Chamber Music at Mount Grace 51
Fade Out 52
John the Cleaner 56
Last to Go 59
Taken as Read 59
Season of Violence 60
Letter 61
The Thing Is 61
Liberal Feature 62
Down to Zero 62
Resistance 63
Conventional Wisdom 64
Returnees 64
Proposition 65
Welcome 65
Between Men 66
The Venice Connection 67

TRANSLATIONS

Charles Baudelaire
        To a Creole 69
        Black Venus 69
        The Albatross 70
        Sailing Home 70
Anon.
        The Concert 71
Eugène N. Marais
        Radio Cradle Song 73
Jean-Joseph Rabearivelo
        Tall Trees 74

INTRODUCTION

This selection contains poems and translations written between the early 1960s when I first began to publish and the present. Of some thirty years' work, this is what I wish to preserve.

They appear in the order in which they were grouped in infrequent slim volumes: *It's about Time* (1974), *Hottentot Venus and Other Poems* (1979), *Love Poems, Hate Poems* (1982) and *Apollo Café and Other Poems* (1989), each of which summarised the output up to the date at which it appeared. In the 1970s, in collaboration with Cecil Skotnes, I published privately several jointly planned combinations of poetry and graphics, like *The Assassination of Shaka* (1974); a few items from these appear here, but generally the texts were too integrated with the graphics to be published independently. A selection from the most recent solo volume, *Season of Violence* (1992), is included at the end.

The dates of composition, or of first publication in a magazine or journal, usually precede the slim volumes by some years, firstly because I have tended to hoard final drafts until comfortable with them, and then because the business of having them accepted for print is often slow and arduous. No item has not been through this procedure. The order of appearance here is only approximate.

As a safety device in the selection I have relied strongly on the judgment of others, primarily the editors of the journals in which they first appeared. This process of outside evaluation dates from the editors of *Granta* in 1961 through to the editor of *PN Review* today. Thus over the years I have become indebted to the poetry editors of many publications: *New Coin, Contrast, Transatlantic Review, Purple Renoster, Bolt, Standpunte, Donga, New Classic, Staffrider, Okike, Ariel, Meanjin, Kunapipi, Wasafiri* and others, through to *London Review of Books*. I have abided by their decisions.

In 1973 Douglas Livingstone selected the work for that first volume in the Mantis Editions, and I have been guided by his criteria since then. Items which have been anthologised I could have fewer doubts about.

Almost all the previous volumes originated with one publisher David Philip in Cape Town – and have been distributed by others elsewhere; in this I have been singularly fortunate. Over a strenuous period Marie Philip as copy-editor has been my mainstay, the ultimate adviser. I have relied on her.

To all of these: my permanent gratitude.

Only once in the exercise of the main activity of my life – writing poetry – have I been able to live off it. This was for a period in 1982 when, as a guest of the Literature Board of the Australia Council, I received a monthly stipend to be a 'poet in residence' there. In Australia I learned that the normal career for one of their poets includes the publication of a *Selected Poems* by age thirty, with five-yearly updates thereafter. In South Africa, where publishing and patronage systems are less confident and developed – and the productive life of a poet (to put none too fine a point on it) is often harassed, subject to the state's interventions, and careers are often short or stifled – only a handful of poets writing in English has put out a *Selected Poems* at all. Some have had to wait for their heirs and executors to do the job; hardly one has made it before hitting thirty. In my case: fifty. Better late than posthumous.

If asked to summarise what I feel my main preoccupations in poetry have been up to this great divide, I would have to reply: love and apartheid. The interrelationship between the two has been my chief subject-matter (what else could it have been?). About this blessing-curse there is a limited amount to be said, which probably accounts for the slender sum-total, and hence the delay in reaching the watershed of having a *Selected Poems* out.

If asked for the main mode: there are two – the lyric and the satire, never disconnected one from the other. The lyrical serves to be assertive, the satirical defensive. The effect of this combination is transgressive, or at least I hope it is. I have never felt myself at home with the givens of any particular historical moment as it has occurred in South African life, so my impulse has been to write against it.

All that said and done, my function has been to remain devoted to finding ways in which poetry itself may continue to express alternatives to unsatisfactory conditions. This I see not as a right given me, but as a duty to be performed. Although this sense of duty has taken many twists and turns over the years, I have not now fallen into the temptation of rewriting any of the work to fit conveniently into the present.

The book concludes with some new poems, all dated 1991-2. One of them, 'The Venice Connection', is addressed directly to my poet friend Armando Pajalich, to whom the whole is dedicated. He taught me the value of translation, so a few translated poems are included to complete the selection.

S. G.
Johannesburg

Stephen Gray: SELECTED POEMS 1960–92

THE DISCOVERY

for Alexis Preller

The Portuguese had beards in those days,
ships and spinnakers pulling South,
keels and crosses built of wood, and all
their hands were held out somehow.

We know how and why they came, and we
know words like 'piccanin'. But what
caused them to feel Africa is dark?
There are temples, the narrow-waisted tribes

wear astonishing uniforms, their huts
are painted weirdly, guinea-fowl and cranes
have bright plumage, the leaves in the forest break
up colour, even the rivers change entirely.

Once a painter arrived, and although his
skin was pale, he tanned himself, bought
an old car, drove everywhere
to show that Africa isn't dark.

(1965)

SNAKE

Snake on the stoep
vertebrae sprung
fangs like boils
jawbone unslung

lecherous hydrant
hissing dramas
what do you know of me
here in my pyjamas

time to withdraw
quit my sack
she's out today
never coming back.

SUNFLOWER

Poor sunflower, your
neck so stretched and
drooping to your feet

can't see the mossies
can't see your own
glory reflected around

sentenced to death
dropping seed in plastic
bags, it's all over

like the hanged man
Pretoria Central
Wednesday dawn.

ZEBRA

Zebra has electric hair
striped in black and white

generates a striking kick
integration on the hoof

blowing off like dynamite
holding more than he can bare

there's a stallion there's a mare
foaling how they breed

overblown it makes you sick
how they sow their stripy seed

powerhouse you stay aloof
Zebra Zebra gallop east

west north especially south
suck the air in with your mouth

we need your type to settle here
to crop the grass at least.

THE TAME HORSES OF VREDEDORP

Their realm is from Piel's Sausage Wholesale
the Fresh Produce market at the cooling towers
skidding on onion skin and tar under M1
to No Animal Drawn Vehicles by Brixton
Tower residential area I tell you a slum

down the Rand they shuffle past Phineas
McIntosh children's park they used to play
centaurs in the old days out for spoils
horses and men raiding over to Langlaagte
taking off over fences and clover with our girls

past the clipped mown green and the Indian gravel
pits dropping off mielies for black bus queues
and then over Church Street Bridge and then
door to door the hawker yelling man
like five for a bob's back in commerce again

they wear horseshoes for luck blinkers bells the lot
shafts bend with them snort in their nosebags
you can hear Pegasus rising from the fumes
stirring flies he travels high on octane
stabled at sunset curried by golden grooms

no chances the tame horses trot pulling carts
back to Vrededorp sammy's in a hurry now
his whip slamming like a chariot race
at the lights it's the Mayfair cavalry
trampling ghettos enemies of the state

shame you'd think they'd let a gelding retire
on the highveld where lucerne's so high but
that sack of worms knock-kneed shrunken-withered sight
makes a last obliging haul past Piel's Wholesale
to the abattoir mark X on his forehead and Petz-D-Lite.

ROUNDING THE CAPE

We're upside down and the Beast is our pilot
scurvy bloats us past all recognition

our navigational tables and the astrolabe
keel over trying to scare us down

we throw our dead at the armour
plated Cape of No Good Storms

there's no hope in losing our Atlantic
I don't declaim about brave stout hearts

Hottentots had ambushes no lettuce
we are not much charmed by ignorance

and now this swing of terrible night
blacking out the simple Southern Cross

with an old titan moaning older threats
from under moustaches of combers

I don't believe in goodwill trade plenty
it's hard to tack around and try.

** O you, the boldest folke*
That ever in the world great things assayed.

THE HORNY CREW

1652 – Van Riebeeck sailed the ocean blue

The early settlers came with manly lust
they've been coming ever since or bust

Indiamen called at the Cape for skin
there was no other bay to drop their anchors in

on unofficial journeys from the Castle to the kraal
they drained the Flats and populated Paarl

their policy was notable for ravages
it quietens things to shoot the noble savages

but every pioneer who left his burning seed
contributed his worth to a brand new breed

admire the way those puritans were forthright
exploring the dark continent at night

face to face with primitive reality
no words of love the Beast admits carnality

on Sundays they ignore the servants' quarters
go to church without their yellow sons and daughters.

FATTER THAN THEY KNEW

O to be in Britain
if it is still there – folk song

In eighteen sweet and twenty
where the sun would never stop
they planted flags in the land of plenty
and sold the Beastly crop

saved up souls in mission stations
counting merinos in their sleep
did their best to break the nations
nobody's knowing the troubles I heap

still my skin is white and strange
my haloed neck is bloody red
I'm turning blue in winds of change
it isn't like Home Office said

old soldiers never die
they tell you how it should have been
clubbed to death with memory
going to London to tell the Queen.

CECIL JOHN

And I am black, but O! my soul is white – Blake

Cecil John your Beast's a hollow English rose
with rings on your fingers and bells on your toes

his pipedream was of diamonds in the empty hinterland
Kimberley was opened as God's gentle mud was panned

Cecil John was witness at the washing of the spears
paid them to be ants to disembowel De Beers

when he struck the map northwards and peered into the mist
veins of gold clinked and blood shot from his fist

blood of others flooding from Zimbabwe to his banks
he bled the bastards white for which we give thanks

Our Lady of the Chartered Co patron of slaves
your little mineboys can only dig graves

your grace presided with a necklace of the hanged
chokers of greed sentencing the damned

Our Lady of the mineshafts enjoy your fairy pleasure
they're interested in heaven in all your earthly treasure

and as you're ascending wrapped in your gold
we kiss your bequest the biggest hole in all the world.

BEAUTY TAMES THE BEAST

A terrible beauty is born – Yeats

Beauty was born through the breakers of oil
she rose in plastic sandals on our soil

see her gaudy apparition on the beach
with a doomboom and a siren screech

she summoned the Beast and newborn birds
to listen to the judgment of her words

her radiance of the apocalypse
outshone South Africa's eclipse

with the Beast in the shade of a sacrificial tree
she leant his badly temper on her knee

she'd fallen out of atomic mutation
her pure eyes were doors of perception

she smoothed the world down in thrall
and a good time was had by all

and so the Beast was tamed with love
the talcum of her words fell finely from above

all the while planning on a new Atlantis
she ate him like a praying mantis

so ends our history of sorrow
her ends are recorded in tomorrow.

SPECIMEN

Under the lens of God's sun
between onion skins of veld and sky
locked between oceans closing south
we avoid His scrutiny

about our microscopic designs
in suspended animation
we function as we do
in holy segregation

see the blacks' warm blood
caking in the squeeze
what upsets their rectitude
noble on their hands and knees

as for God's own puritans
trying hard to multiply
inheritors of parasols and hats
down on the beach to braai

when the sky opens up
and the tweezers are meant
to pick me for example
will I be magnificent.

IT'S ABOUT TIME

It's about time we talked in words
not cash principles group areas
developments effluent slick
words you can hear me say

about time we walked on earth
not concordes state limousines
saracens water or hell
on earth that connects you with me

about time we worked on the heart
not cancer computers banks
explosions inflations thromboses
the heart of blood in you and me

time we made time you know
not fences colours legislation
heritage separation progress
time about you and time about me

now I must tell you I love you
not dirty books censorship love
divorces my former love war
I love you and it's about time.

WOLRAAD WOLTEMADE

The lightning that bolted the sails of the *Jonge Thomas*
            in Table Bay
to the continental shelf with a ship's cat's amplified
            howl in the rigging
with capsizal into the reefs of drink a bottoms-up welcome
            in a port of call
was the rock and roll of a neptune gone vengeful
            with lay me down
and like to die fury – o the spray in the crow's nest
            and cackle on deck –
electrifying passengers and crew alike they were all
            in like distress

was to the safe pasteurized milkman of Woodstock
                    an illumination
that a ship of state could be so perishable so uncaulked
                    by natural forces
that with a perfect excuse he broke off
                    his daily round
spurred his mount out of the sidestreets for once
                    and into the sea
where traction was a matter of musculature and breath
                    the kiss of life
he'd dreamed of and rescue a tide of thrown-up medals
                    for man and stallion

except that the non-swimmers tailing on the horsehair
                    of his return journeys
through the echo chambers of brine to the soaking beach
                    pair after pair
were too choked for gratitude and the eighth evacuation
                    was too much
clutching on the bridle for the waterline to sustain
                    this heavy ferry
so that as the ribs and rivets blew on rescuer and panicking
                    deeply out of depth
he could only be sure all things are possible before
                    the kelp takes over.
                                        (1773-1973)

SIREN

The last capitalist lady
sings on the rocks over rubble

We were wrong all along
we made a mistake

her teats exude Ambre Solaire
but she has no baby to suckle

those are flashbulbs that were her eyes
her thighs are juicy with grief

We were wrong all the time
we got it all wrong

her teeth are shockingly clean
there's no one left where she's been

she has a push-button navel
her shoulders light up like wings.

EGGS

O Johnny with a pair of eggs
shacked up between his legs

what's he going to do with all that juice
throw it in hell let heaven loose

O but he's purely white
cracking his shells in the dead of night

what's he going to do with all that man
bleach the sheets with albumen

O he has a dream of his native land
lying upside down with outstretched hand

Poor Johnny's got the secret of life
doesn't want to share it with a knife

Johnny hears the pitch black drum
breaks in a sweat as the colours run.

HOMECOMING

He's had no time to let youth slacken
to let his own destiny awaken
it has to be, that kind of thing happens

there's no tradition to impair his action
he wrestles the crowd to his satisfaction
from Germiston returning to Athens

he's the son of peasants, emigrated
thinks the classics overrated
it has to be, that kind of thing happens

he has no sentiment about all that's sacred
tips the porter more than he expected
from Germiston returning to Athens

a Greek-South African's home once more
let the landslide strip his psyche raw
it has to be, that kind of thing happens
from Germiston returning to Athens.

ISANDHLWANA

Saddle Mountain is a seat for a large god
who sits up there going nowhere – washing his feet

in the stream like a horseshoe stamping the ground –
he has time on his hands to remember by

he recalls the day a whole British army bowed down
to eat the red soil they had come to claim

he knows how the dying impis
roasted horses to last one more night

but nobody climbs up for stories anymore
life's gone dull and so has the glory.

BATTLEHILL

If you feel that there are ghosts here
on a cold night – maybe under a circled moon

ghosts that cluster and go about their business
reforming shrieking charges driven by

an old way of killing against a new invasion
– as happened here lest we forget –

notice that as dawn breaks like a live shroud
and the memorials turn out to be anthills

that doesn't mean you are to be relieved yet
as night comes down and the sights are set.

CATARACT

In good times the river knows
no obstacle no inhibition – it can

rise from its bed in plentiful
forward abundance and hover

until the clutch of gravity
plants it on down further on

in bad times there is no telling
how potent it used to be

bad times are hard on the earth
when barriers hold up like death.

QUARRY

It's a matter of rocks peeling down
at the pressure point and the temptation

to say this valley driven into a pool
sliding down its own pleasurable flanks

resembles something human and personal
a secret zone that shouldn't be exposed

but that's sheer romantics because
this wall pounded at by drills

is only an industrial concern
a store for easy detonation.

VELDFIRE

There's no averting the kind of gale
that smears fire beneath it

no deflecting the hopscotch flames
storming from low ravines to the sky

and if the grass is skinned painfully
stropped across like a razor

and firebrands burst like bombshells
and sirens go as if it's doomsday

hold on – because tomorrow
it turns black and grey and green.

TOTEMS

In regarding totems as alien presences
that pull down the sky on you

do not be overawed by their linkage
of knees to earth and earth to heaven

they pray for us even when we're not involved
they are always there like old stumps

attracting the sunlight with indifference
balancing the plain like hubs

and when in a fever you stumble once more
on totems they connect you back to the world.

A SOUTH AFRICAN CHRISTMAS

Although we celebrate
Christmas upside down
although for us it's hot as fire
when it should be cold
for us the days are long as waking
when they should be short
and we are scattered in pleasure
when we should be cosily indoors

although we celebrate Christmas
with surfing and skydiving
        instead of red-nosed reindeers
and the red red robin is out-
numbered by a network of
        summer swallows
the Christmas trees shimmer
with shining dust instead of snow
and the sleigh-bells are really
icecream lorries coming
        through mirages

although for us this day is a
regular day of hostilities
        instead of peace
and Christmas puddings are heavy
as landmines and holly
        is like barbed wire
although with us the news today
was of increased tension
        and no relief
and the herald angels sing
carols of warning and caution
        instead of joy

there are still some good things
we do have in common
        with all people
like cattle and sheep coming
home to a kraal and a bright
        star to steer by
like the birth of new children
born to suffer born to
        die for us
and the sure possibility of
three wise men who bear goodwill
        brotherhood and understanding

cattle and sheep returning home
to a stable in a simple
        routine
and the virgin and child perpetually
insisting that we do
        have a chance
that Christmas is for all women

and men in all seasons
        in all places
and that the earth we belong to
prefers new birth and life
        to death.

MAYFAIR

O suburb of stripped cars & highrise hollyhocks
    where the greater unemployed
swat sweat that crawls like flies down fallen legs
    where cataracted chickens gawp
from turning spits in Costa's Terminus Café
    where housewives vie on volume
down a one-way street flushed with soap-opera
    & their potato-fat serving girls
shine the Dandy polish on their red knees

backyard archaeology turns up a shard
    plastic rattles glass coal
& the condensed milk throat of the neighbour's
    bat-eared military son
breaks all siesta on his A minor bugle practice
    the jackpot days are over for
the Dixi-Cola pensioners in the Thursday
    post-office payout queue
decay like rope around their contoured necks

the mother's clinic scrapes a formless arm with vaccine
    tetanus is in the wind
scabby wild cats track their corrugated clawy paths
    to the bins of the Limosin Hotel
& miners from Frelimo stroll in unofficial gangs
    against the menace of stick em up & defence
& trespass on the Gaza Strip where Reggie and Honey
    packing through Majestic Mansions
deny all knowledge all involvement in crime

down the plane-tree Ninth Avenue rides a blue nun
    on a cross-barred bicycle
down the brick of the Dolphin Street swimming pool
    loiter kids held up by candy floss
down the intersection bounce Clover Dairies icecream
    sidecars & bells of appetite
down the coach-house whitewash plunge rust and creeper
    & the ritual taxi ride to church
rounds a Pentecostal Sunday curve towards heaven

O Mayfair & a Chinaman's chest flat as a slime-tray
        parades the verandas of concrete waggon wheels
how uplifting! – the pumpkins on roofs still
        the TRG car come for southern flesh
& Mr Fonseca Builder unclasps his racing pigeons
        to spiral over smallness & the dumps
the fine golden sand the cyanide lagoon the synagogue
        the alcoholic pavements & knives & curlers
into undefeated clarity of the whitest air.

AFAR IN THE DESERT

Bush-boy speaks

He loves to ride afar in the Desert
with the silent Bush-boy by his side

he does not demand that I speak to him
break the melancholy of his exile

he's never grown out of his Native Land
he does not look as if he belongs

here we offer him a kingdom of all
he surveys down the sight of a firelock

an Eden puckered with bare spoor
over the border and into the dark

but this man – he rides in excursions
looking back through me for home

he says it is wrong to enslave me
yet he grows taller in my company

he says he writes poems for freedom
he does not hear me sing in my chains

I sing with the battering of hoofs
sing until it's unbearable to him

I will keep silent if my master wishes
there is no bad spleen in me

I will not disturb his luxury
while he feels he rides alone

silent by my side afar in the Desert
I will never let you go.

HOTTENTOT VENUS

My name is Saartjie Baartman and I come from Kat Rivier
    they called me the Hottentot Venus
they rang up the curtains on a classy peepshow two pennies
    two pennies in the slot and I'd wind up
shift a fan and roll my rolypoly bum
    and rock the capitals of Europe into mirth
I was a special voluptuary a squealing passion
    they had never seen anything like it before
Little Sarah twenty six born on the vlei past Grahamstown
    bought for a song and a clap of the hands
a speculative sketch come to life a curiosity
    of natural science weighed measured
exported on show two pennies two pennies
    in the Gallery of Man I am unique
I am lonely now I always was out here
    my deathbed a New Year's eve
a salon couch girdled with reporters and I turned
    my complexion to the wall and dreamed
of a knife cutting deep in a springbok's hide
    and they woke me with brandy for smelling salts
and I wouldn't wake again in their august company
    my soul creeps under cairns where
wayside travellers throw another stone in my memory
    two pennies two pennies dropped on my eyes
they laid me in state in my crinoline robe
    my hands folded coyly as they always were
and I let them bury my body so celebrated so sensational
    they could never do while I was alive
what they wanted to do sink me in wax and decant my brain
    and put me in a case in the Museum of Man
I stare out at the Eiffel Tower my hands covering
    my vaginal flaps my own anomaly
the kneebone connected to the thighbone connected to
    the hipbone connected to the spine and the skull
they mounted me without beads or skins or quivers
    Saartjie Baartman is my name and I know
my place I know my rights I put down my foot
    and the Tuileries Gardens shake I put down
my foot and the Seine changes course I put
    down my foot and the globe turns upside down
I rattle my handful of bones and the dead arise.

SONG OF THE GOLD COMING IN

Over a brutal landmass I hover
at night like an ear of corn
bending across your attraction

many's the scalding circle
I make around day and night
always drawing in for you

some say I'm aflame just for you
I was always destined for you
but many say that at me

I'm young enough to be choosy
I don't mind circuiting for ever
I'm untouchably beautiful

burning and rolling so slim
what a piece of tail you say
my light makes even you adorable

but now I'm helpless I fall
I'm raining fire I can't hold
I shall pock all your skin

I sink on your stomach
your chest on your teeth
I'm like sweat lightening you

o and I stroke you so hot
was there ever such a crashlanding
you're drawing me down take me

into your innermost cavern
bury me deep I'm ashamed
I'm broken I am no more

I belong to you now
I can feel your heart shift
I know I must love you now

but some say I was always yours
I never corroded stayed contrary
thrown out from your depths

I suppose you try and void me
belch me out in forges of lava
hurl me about like pus

but I lie in your armpits and groin
always resistant always me
as indigestible as a saint

and you dark cannibal whom I
love throw me out throw me
out from your burning guts

so I rest here for always
like a chain at your neck
or a warm sun on your earlobes

watching you guarding you
making you rich every moment
until you stop hating me.

SONG OF THE RAIDERS

We came always deviously but in a great tradition
like many who'd failed before us looking for gold

we always knew there were gold and slaves for the taking
study our unreliable but optimistic maps of Africa

our forefathers I suppose were successful like Jason
lading up for home with glittering skins piled on deck

but I knew it was always where Solomon for all his wisdom
never knew past Pharaoh's head on the Sheba route

we had evidence that Abyssinia and Sudan poured
gold like a waterfall shaped in a rainbow

we had evidence that over the Atlas Mountains
gold fairly walked around like crocodiles or hippo

that was when the Niger and Benin cast whole huts
by the lost wax method in sheerest gold

and when we steered by that touching rumour of Prester John
who not only beat his piazzas and bedsteads of gold
        but was Christian

and all simple rivers and unconfirmed reports pointed down
further down on the Arab routes now which was intolerable

and all was a blazing vision of golden kingdoms of Ophir
and Zimbabwe guarded by immortal gem-laden women
        and stone vultures

so we came disguised as Portuguese navigators peeling
the globe like an orange but as you know way off target

and we came as the Dutch who settled for silver and copper
(never quite trusting their talents against a dark inland)

and we came again once the Spanish doubloon competed
with our fair sails upon the fairest Cape as the British

and the rest you know how the whole white Transvaal cut back
like a piecrust and a basin of gold was revealed

we keep raiding for that although our names may change
the gold once you've struck it you know never does.

IN MEMORIAM: OLIVE SCHREINER

1

You choose to outdo the living
buried on a koppie a mile high
with a world's view over blue simmering horizons
it took twelve porters three days to haul
your coffin up these greasy slopes
to pack you away in a dome of rock
taking Buffelskop as your natural cathedral
and you the lightning conductor

we worked at it all morning to reach you
with a survey map cameras and packs
and in your honour braaied lunch in clouds
of herb-smelling fire alongside your sarcophagus
there's not much to say to the close dead
one functions normally
a trifle embarrassed

and although not one of us was superstitious
we had to admit it was eerie
in the vast gathering of thermals
that the shade of a lammervanger
should crisscross us up there
symbolizing your kind of freedom
probably watching from its height for prey.

2

It is easy to picture the obsessive you were
Olive sprawling out pages in her teenage
stuck on an African farm
Olive demanding her rights of a baffled storekeeper
Olive in the dusty evenings striding the riverside
Olive thumping her pupils in a fit of pique
Olive choking obesely on gulps of air
Olive trying to fly but getting lead-lined
Olive the scandalous outspoken liberal
that we can no longer be

Or Olive in a late-night stupor
stoked up like the train at Matjiesfontein
hauling the public down the tracks of
a war a woman's right an atrocity
a conscience of a nation that never knew

and always with a humour no one else could afford
your curly Germans fake Brits and frozen Lyndalls
your sexy troopers and laborious whores
your wearing a pith-helmet among ostriches
your burying yourself higher than Cradock
higher than Cecil Rhodes
higher than South Africa.

3
We each make our own gestures towards you
unsure of the formalities
but quite cheerful in our hearts
and as the sun shifts over
the scrub ignites with sweat
the rocks shine out like iron slides
and we skid down to the derelict land below

it was good to have neared you
good to know.

FERNANDO PESSOA

The scholar of Mozambique / stepped from Durban
High with an unusual decorum / a natty classical
verve in quest of a sea-lens boy / with a glass thigh

no tropical fervour bore / his symbolic fruit
but a patient fragmentation / of the brain
in libraries decked in nightingales / and smut

once the persona had gone / he cast a dozen
others in his point of focus / the metaphysical
the patriotic the sceptical / and always the lover

who never recovered his whole / assimilating
banter despite the tendons / of his holding Portuguese
as his tongue touched a hot knee / and spattered.

DIVERS, REUNION ISLAND

From the concrete jetty jump
        one two ten children
into a pale space out of gravity
        buckle like hinges on
impact with the bomb-shell sea –
        a zone of volleyballs &
belly-flops & inflated tubes
        is claimed by each of them –
despite their various-coloured origins
        the thrust across the open sky
the plunge over the sloppy wave
        grabs them down the same –
& the preteen muscle games always
        land in nuzzles down the reef
& gasps & bursting salty eyes –
        they wade ashore glistening –
the dark prefect points in a child
        kicked beyond the perimeter –
the tame black half-Alsatian dog
        charges with a new batch brakes
as they go over holding noses hands air
        aloft & legs awry before they
crash inevitably downwards yet again –
        one girl's hair pulls across
the peel of the lagoon like a spider –
        the less defiant contemplate
the fish beneath the squeaking lilo
        whose eyes enlarge such beings
into the dumb thunder of invasion –
        the black dog barks decides
the golden-headed baby may prop
        her small bikinied hip on his
warm fur his over-excited side –
        there is no end to children
diving off the jetty evermore
        no end to shaping summer
in your own image perpetually.

LOCAL HISTORY

In this hunched low seaside resort
        crusted in leisure and dough
(the riots continue elsewhere out of reach
        the fishermen trawl for no fish)
I sit and compose myself to write

and as I sit and compose myself here
        (the riots continue
the fishermen fish out the end of the sea)
        and as I compose and
sit and write a history of local endeavour

(the riots continue to flourish out there
        there are no fish in the sea)
cramped in leisure and fed up on dough
        I sit and compose myself
for the time when you burn like a shoal on me.

BIRTH OF A SEAL

Once you won't believe it this bay
        was ground up by blue whales
underwater was a starfish warble of converse
        from Gordon's Bay to Simon's Town
and bounced out past Agulhas beam to beam

and seals cartwheel reminiscently in diesel
        oil on troubled waters
only the other day one posed belly up
        for photographs on the quay
shrugging out her afterbirth to applause

her confidence away from the bask
        of her fellow unprotected seals
swam through all demarcation between air
        and water bringing right to our feet
one large-eyed pelt for us to wear.

THE SUICIDE

Meanwhile the waves pillage on
    the Dalebrook shore
a hazy cross-referral of troubles
    a double-decker fall-out
a skid into a sand disposal

meanwhile the SA Police off
    border duty are searching
the beach for a suicide case
    last night in his manic way
he walked out of it out on the bay

and now before they find evidence
    every bottle carries a message
every arm of seaweed an Omega wristwatch
    every shell a rolling eye
but that's it folks he's disappeared.

TO A YOUNG POET

You arrive with a treasured hoard of poems
    stashed in your pocket
write them out in a daze on a scrap-pad
    I watch you hunched over
offering the lines across to me (waiting

breathless) while I read what I've seen alas
    a hundred times before
these poor jewels need cutting and polishing
    need to be set by you
I can break you by telling you why

I could also tell you that the heart
    is only another muscle
when loneliness swells it's your own to kill
    when a poem's yours
you'll know it my boy you really will know.

POETRY READING

You come to hear him break his heart
     and break yours as well
you come to watch him laugh it off
     and watch him watching you
you come because you think it's true

and he the object of your exact attention
     looks out at your glasses
flashing like stars and your awkward
     postures that reflect souls
and wonders if you're really over there

because the gap between you and him
     widens and gapes and soars
so that every cluster in the good audience
     bounces back the message that
the more he talks the more he lies.

MERMAID

Then there was the mermaid with
     a skull of seagrass
and great difficulty hobbling into the house
     she held only death
as a truly intense lifelong companion

I wondered what shape for her death assumed
     to lure such a high-pitched
siren off her rock and into a coil
     of scaly gillflap
it was that strange mammalian fellow

besotted on his conquest of all of her
     fingering her tummy and web
clenching his fist and she stretched on his tan
     in blotchy hopeful colours
cooled by his bloodstream just visible.

MOTHER AND SON

A species of praise in a housewife's age
        this is for a distressed
mother of a son twice her own size
        there in whose face
is contained the shadow of her look

within his diffident hands lurk your
        nervous bitten fingers
within his chest beats a round heart
        you feel but you cannot see
within his slow eyes ferret your concerns

he contains you though you sulk inside
        ache and bulge like a growth
a reversal of the way he came from you
        into the expanse of his being
would deliver you too to gasp and splutter out.

GRAND PARADE, SEPTEMBER 1976

There's a malfed schoolkid rising
        with a garbage lid shield
Achilles in miniature burnt
        with anger outfacing
the emergency shortwave cops

teargas spatters around his sandals
        corroding his tongue
and he bangs the storm with a cymbal
        applauding with one hand
(the grapeshot next for hail

the FN for lightning of the gods)
        and because he is only human
his fury cries out that only man
        must prevail not
metal not masks not thunderers.

ADAMASTOR'S NEW YEAR BULLETIN, 1976-7

O my people this is going to be a bad year
    you've heard my doomcast before
take heed of my spilling of unrest
    for God will never change
your souls without their really changing

at sunrise we pray for you
    in the land of the hippo
the land of the R1 and Star 45
    the Alouette pouring
down gas for the lungs of the people

we pray in our tear-sodden voices
    that the helmets and batons hold
that the barbed-wire keeps in the prisons
    that the dawn may not come
without knuckles and lamp-posts and fear

we pray for the Phantoms and Hotshots
    heeling havoc underfoot
spidering over the lawn of beige
    cueing your heads across
to roaring hungry Alsatians

for the Mongrels patrolling in gangs
    blue with resinous juices
cutting you down in your asbestos suits
    flamethrowing down arcades
cleaning out all ash of housewives

and for the stalags invested with bankers
    we pray you shall make it
as the Rothschilds withdraw their investment
    the vaults fill with debit
and securities char beyond recognition

from Angola to Zambezi a plague on
        your shuttered white houses
may you be circled by man-eating sharks
        may your air fill with the drone
of repeating machine-guns like rain

may your sanitary belts fester
        with landmines like boils
and your trenches be greedy for death
        may war blacken your walls
and you stick in the throat of your bugles

may all that befalls you this season
        as you turn in mad circles
to gnaw at your guts like a leopard
        strewing out poison
be your own people's happy new year.

THOMAS BOWLER'S KALK BAY

One watercolour day of rock and swell
        (in eighteen hundred and sixty)
there where strandlopers now pick
        the green crevices for bait
stood a Victorian governess with a

lone child of Anglican elegance
        two pale strokes for legs
and a bubble of soft breeze for joy
        her hat held imperiously
over her isolated childish head

her security across the reaches
        was a British forest of
masters in Simon's Bay locking
        bows in a cluster of defence
black penstrokes on aquamarine.

MY FATHER'S WATERCOLOUR, 1918

His perspective of the coast across the bay
        was not wrong
nor of the yellow rocks by green sea
        there were less houses then
to colour in around Kalk Bay

the page shines through the wash today
        showing the sky pale
the caught sea tangles with the fibre
        of changing paper
just as his young vision has altered

what I would like to know is
        can a comparison be made
between what he saw there and then
        and what I see now
through his younger optimistic eyes.

OUTRIDING

And tonight I'll dream of riding
        horses over grey sand
as low tide withdraws a mirror
        on which your thoroughbred
shoes crunch at an easy pace

the foxy chestnut cowboy shaps
        clap on the barrel chest
and your stirrups shine upside
        down and your horse's soft
foamy muzzle prods sloppily at mine's

and sandpipers reverse over the flat
        and knees rubbing we veer
into a gallop down level and plash
        it out hell for leather
jockey-wise high in the saddle

and that fudgy sand thuds up
        through pastern and fetlock
and the martingale keels forward
        on one leg at a go
and nervous terns reel away

and even the kelp stands up
        in the furious swell
and trumpets in deep unison
        and bluebottles pop
on impact and the spooked

snuffling steam-engine ride
        of a runaway victory
ends in a hockslide of spray
        and sand and old wreckage
cast right up to the face

and after that riding back home
        snorting and covered in sweat
we're overextended perhaps and the
        dunes slide beneath
and the last exhausted vault over reeds

lands us exercised a bit grazed
        but extremely game for
the slow pack-up ritual
        the sawdust stableyard
the rubdown with an old sackcloth

and a late methodical brush down
        cold flanks and a comb
on the mane and a gentle
        return to a small paddock
and not forgetting the last sugarlumps.

NO WAY

Now I've replaced you let the
        years take you and
someone not unlike you engages
        me almost completely
but by mistake you're still there

if the door knocks I don't mean to
        but there's your son hurling
himself on my head and my hand
        closing my ear for him
not to fall down it yelling 'No Way

No Way you're not my Daddy'
        or bend at table to
fetch a run-away pea and come up
        and brush her hand and say
your name you're always so clumsy.

LETTER TO HER HUSBAND

There's no way you can understand
        how deeply I envy
your legal right to walk with her
        through the harbour
holding her legalised hand

for us behind your back there is
        the furtive planning on
vacant flats to occupy for
        an hour of illicit
loving fit to kill us both

and after that we retreat side
        by side in public
unable to show that in the air
        between our warm bodies
ghostly fingers try to hold on.

LOVE POEM, HATE POEM

Now of all cruel times loving seems
        a guilty luxury
why when I look forward to
        pouring dry inside your arms
should I ring bells and trigger alarms

I would rather the sirens called for you
        and that when a line pulled straight
urgently telling all those I hate
        to slacken their dreadful hold
another line could be about only you

as time clicks by like a grenade
        a fuse of crackerjacks
passions exhaust their casings
        and a kiss bangs into fire
and loving you becomes their obliteration.

HOW COULD YOU FORGET?

There is no obvious comment to make anymore
        as the love that contained me
for you was a trap so please
        say no more say
no more I *know* what you mean

but for me the dialogue goes on
        and all that we never said
due to inadequate planning due to
        inexpressible hopeful
delusions and quick bedroom farces

remains silent before the flapping curtain
        there's no farewell musak
no fine climax and slamming of doors
        oh how could you forget
but you could and that's now the end of it.

LAST TRAIN

The trains that howl in the night
        howl for you you know
the victims of unearthly blues
        howl a bit for you
they miss you as much as I do

I have to drag them all into the act
        because I find it hard to say
that they all unknowing can express
        what I can't express
blowing hooters round dark corners

passengers pressed on upright seats
        submitting to transports
paying to get where they're going
        when they'd rather have stayed
at home beneath the weight of you.

THE FUNCTION OF POETRY

Poems are written after the act
        the decisive second
which the hours in memory learn
        to articulate over
the boundary into their shape

they happen between the perception
        and the urge to perform
a way of recording what's already been
        they're a poor substitute
for the precise experience that occurred

for example today I conceived a manner
        of stretching a poem across
from this book to your complicated lap
        I knew the way and its reach
but when I'd the movement you'd gone.

UNDERWATER MUSIC

When you're hung over very concerned
        where you place your feet
your arms hugging air your tummy bare
        making for the rock pool
and the more gracious sway of the swell

and I'm alongside skidding like a bird
        scared of curious people
hitting the water hides so much
        we can butt and stroke and
probe as if we had greater concerns

under the water where one-eyed
        frogmen don't expect
codes of affection and the limewash walls
        reflect togetherness
only we in our secrecy understand.

CORRESPONDENCE

But loving you is a matter of
        familiar details coming alive
wrinkles under your eyes from grinning
        warm hands and cold feet
a haunch like a saddle horn and

intakes of breath your face cream
        your gold filling
the way your tongue clicks your lip
        it's the way your knee
hangs out for steadiness on a cotton

sheet pulling down on our heads
        anywhere anytime
these things are unique and personal
        they sustain our closeness more
than the opening of a thousand envelopes.

THE WITNESS

The cat witness decided out of
        sheer curiosity
breaking the habit of long shyness
        abandoning her retreat
to investigate what was going on

like a black-and-white nun coming
        out of her innocence
she pawed and probed her wet nose
        in unseemly naughtiness
purring with reserve at our lack of

now her pugmarks dry on your back
        your skin shining with claws
her tail left out on my neck
        and having decided she knows
she licks herself and us to sleep.

NIGHT SONG

Sleep gently my love gently for the
        sea like an endless
washing machine and the bosun's whistle
        call for you only too
soon to be contemplated at all

sleep with the warm lather wrung
        like a bell on your belly
the foam on your trim ironed cheek
        and the ghost of a sleeve
caught on the edge of the mattress to dry

dream gently of me as I do of you
        my partner my guide
gently of breath on your recessed nipple
        a narrowing eye and your
slackening flesh winding to a halt.

ASSEMBLAGE

I'm going to have to reconstitute you
        by some good process
it's hard to love my countrymen if you
        being one by extension
are lost and gone from all of me

(O yes I want all of you back)
        start again carefully not many
stanzas to go now not many
        hours left for this kind of
summoning up of the presumed dead

Prospero could do it with his staff
        I doubt if I can the same
poetry has this fine illusion that
        making words can
make the world appear generous again

take it graphically like this
        I have one rock pool
taut as a navel sewn with weed
        I have one octopus
arranged this way and sticking

one red medusa you know the type
        it'll pump at a shock
I have a sea urchin lashed
        with spines that will open
the third day is knocked in your hand

I have Dettol and great wonder drugs
        swabs to clean your scabs
I have above all enough glucose
        to shoot up your wrist
forceps to birthmark your skull

lug your sleeping head my love
        out of the mortar of sand
there's a pillar of fire on the water
        bandages wind out
from coffins of debris towards land

the promontory we cling to anchors
        you on a mother-of-pearl
swing your locks and a clout
        on the sternum starts
the pounding and gasp for cool air

it's all yours my bonanza
        my flourishing offspring
my recurrence of body my love
        it's all yours again
use us gently use us clean.

THE HISTORICAL MOMENT

For once I am not in love not available
To curl your hair on an iron without burning your neck
To heave your car when it won't start in a rush-hour
To smuggle wine under my jacket up the lift to your flat
To cut a rose and pass it to you without scratching your hand

Not being in love and unavailable these days
I don't rush to the phone when it rings and hold it nervously
I don't adjust my collar ten times in case you're looking
I don't save books for you to read pictures to see
In restaurants I don't study the chair alongside

And rush home after work planning what to buy for you
When next you arrive and arrange yourself on the sofa
I breathe more easily with your ear off my heart
No more the babble of stress the hope in a calculated pause
I speak calmly and thoughtfully and forthrightly

Now that I am for once myself again
I chat to the general public in a general way
Read newspapers through to the sports and the classifieds
Find singles are poorly catered for but persevere
Watch families with children and criticise them

All these years of toil and adrenalin and expense
I can hardly remember I've lost my memory
Of how like a mountaineer I'd scale your breath
How within you I'd reach like a serpent and coil
Through a winter inside the warmth of your sleep

Nor in my feelings damaged and scarred
Is the bleeding of that terrible pain
When the blade of an arrow dug through my back
The wound now's a trench a gutter a wrinkle
Being out of love it has healed and grown over

Meanwhile I live in a moment of history
And no telegrams come – there is news only of massacres
The red streets of this city are flushed with blood
They've blown up the powerlines poisoned the water
It's only a matter of time now since love is done.

THE HERB GARDEN

My mother before she died insisted
I should have a herb garden
Something in her English soul
Amid rough South Africans
Called for the tenderness of mint
The old scent of lavender and sage

They arrived in soggy pages of *The Star*
With a spade taller than herself
She dug them into my backyard
Before I was ready for them
A cigarette tightly in her lips
Explaining chives made life worthwhile

That is how she died in her own
Garden of sweet remembrance
Very frail then with a bucket and spade
The size we children used for play
Always finding the sun too hot the soil
Far too dry for the gentler herbs

Today after the long heart-stopping drought
My mother's bed of lost spices
Has so flourished I have cut it back
And the mint is in the crevices of fingers
The sage under my very nails
And I remember her every gesture.

INCIDENT AT PENNINGTON

The beach is calm now and a mud belt
of riversand quells the restless sea.

Earlier at low tide where mussels scale
the exposed rocks in bladed necklaces

a black youth caught in the crossed
off-shore swells struck back like a

fan of panic felt the Mozambique
Current tug up his heels and waist

waves from SE and NE intersect
over his throbbing hopeless head.

Our leonine host stows each morn
in vygies and flamelilies in a milkcrate

a yellow rope with harness and buoy
marked dourly LIFELINE HERE

above the tideline to leash in such
succourless cases so smally lost

in this impersonal loud im-
mensity of surf and sand and wilderness

the recent CP victory declares only
whites may use to save themselves.

But chances of making the *Witness* front-page
from Pennington are all too rare

for Indians and Coloureds and benighted
whites to pass rope hand to hand

while my own God-neglecting fearless dad
is out there tangling the lad back in.

The heat the breakers contradict
and really it is time to pass a person on

like builders bricks or naughty
children sweeties under teacher's stare.

He'd have seen Agulhas before his time
had heroism ne'er become routine.

He shakes his long quivering legs
and gives the broadest smile seen yet

and like two solicitors clinching a
perfect deal they shake on it

my father deferentially and fey
the youth who beat the whole

sea with a finger-tingling shyness
he who might have left no name behind

and not been known to any one of us
and who still is quite unknown.

APOLLO CAFÉ

Always I have meant to write of Apollo Café
Apollo Café has everything you need
Open on Sundays at 9.00 for the news
Open after-hours for bread and milk
On the corner-stand at 6th and Church
Johannesburg S. A. below the ridge
Always I have meant to write of Apollo Café

There are many Apollo Cafés in this poem
Each has his own with blue awnings
And moustaches smoke Winston and Good and Clean
And a catalogue of newslines and braaiwood
And the greased-over windows of curiosity
Packed with last-minute supergoods
Each has his own with overpainted frames

And prams and banana-peels and the City Council bin
And the leak of paraffin from a silver pump
Siphoning the poor juice of a spirit-stove
Between nets of bulbs and a shaking fridge
A necklace of cardboard Outspan oranges
And the sawdust of sandals and boots and straws
Each has his or her own Apollo Café

The corner of commerce in a sluggish suburb
Meeting-place of caught-out consumers
Eggs in design boxes soap soup Coke
Crackers and Mars Bars dope racing forms
Crinkle chips sliced polony biltong and sweat
Condensed milk rusks biscuits instant balloons
Always I have meant to write of Apollo Café

And in this purple city of Johannesburg S. A.
When the jacarandas refine the air with sap
And the roots swell under tarmac pavements
Ready to bunch up the stones for bare feet
And the lethargic cleaner in a wide straw hat
Sweeps blood into a municipal bag that's when
It's time to write about your or my Apollo Café

When the secret life of things can no longer be hidden
When minedust in the eye-duct generates pain
The grass instead of waving and shining crawls forth

And the railway borders tumble up to billboards
Shunting and connected the cattletrucks bellow with heat
Christmas beetles bring down the thunder
That is the time to write of Apollo Café

When the blue Fords of the Brixton Murder and Robbery
Crackle with rape and disaster and greetings
And Allied Publishing drops *Sarie* and *Huisgenoot* in bundles
And the butcher's delivery swings a calf's head
And the black poet's BMW stops for ginger beer
At the refreshment station on a hot afternoon
That is what Apollo Café is there for for ever

Yours or mine it stays while we go by
Apollo Café is a fixture needs a face-lift
Probably isn't even called Apollo Café
Tram Terminus or Springbok or Madeira
Boland or Vyfster or Mixolodeon
On five thousand South African corner plots
But always Apollo Café is what I remember

In Johannesburg S. A. this purple city
Which feeds the hungry and cares for the poor
Which balances the GNP almost daily
Which emanates mercy over the wide land
Which stays a people town and loves the lame and halt
In which I live save my soul
There is always a special Apollo Café

Its yellow-framed door is always open
For pawpaws and litchis and watermelon
For catfood and iced suckers and Marmite
And drinking yoghurt and bubblegum and lard
And cheddar cheese and mousetraps and brooms
Tuna peas bacon butter carrots chops
Matches candles fittings jelly Doom

And despite the reign of avarice and greed
Despite the sweepstakes and the price of gold
The rampant dollar and the declining rand
The pegging of the fuel-line and the ANC
The boycott of arms and sports and plays
Despite the ministers on TV with faces like frogs
At Apollo Café necessity holds sway

For a coin that's devaluing at Apollo Café
You can buy comic books and make a call
Buy liquorice and vetkoek and the wing
Of Farmer Brown and Dreyer's ice-cream
And milkshakes and coconut and samp
And return the empties and collect the tops
For a coin you can insert a silver jukebox tune.

THE SUN ROOM

Under the woven creeper breaks the glare
over a trim kikuyu lawn the sun pours

the white light of a drought-stricken summer burning
warm as a nuclear attack

oh shield your eyes against its intensity
guard as if against a phalanx of flash-bulbs

with the melting heat over vegetation
why have I tried to write this poem before?

in the bleached perpetual paleness
I imagine for I cannot properly see

the details of a well-kept garden a pool
a Kreepy-Krawly doing time a lilo half gone

a metal table with the end of wineglasses crusts
a coffee-pot the shell of a sausage a melon-rind

and a bluebottle circuiting the wreckage of my kind
and the filter eating doses of chlorine

why this tranquil Northern Suburbs scene
when it should be a terrible one of war?

but this is what they're fighting for these days
the property that bows to lazy worship

the red-and-white striped umbrella
the Malawi print sarong pressed on the tiles

presently the privileged will appear
with sunglasses like mine around the Penguin like me

with a skin peeling back on a torture of flesh
bloodshot eyes joints swollen with sunburn

and the slow wipe of a sun-screening agent
preventing X-rays of sensitive shy places

this is the postmodern dilemma South African-style
in love with the good life but loathing the means

ten thousand of the exploited have worked for me
to have this incredible sun-crazy abandon

I can hardly feel guilty about it
after ice-cream and strawberries and liqueur

if I roll an underexposed hip upwards
Late Harvest courses to the back of my throat

if I rearrange myself upon my guts
Christmas pudding squeezes into acid

the spirit is only too connected to the body
and the body knows the pleasures of its greed

and thus there is no thinking past this poem
tangled head forward I sink into the blue water

let it take me like a problem in physics
arrange specific gravity so I come out on top

the sun throws assegais through the liquid
in strange distortions it becomes tangible

and planetary bubbles whirl in disorder
I am my own self enveloped in light

I am the coral and the fish the curve
of a whale's fin on the deep graze

I am only bone and flesh and nerve and hair
sprung from the sun's sheath into bursting air

and just because this is my poem I'm breaking through
because it is mine to maintain or change

I now turn off the sun erase this decor
we are you and I for once alone

in the sombre bushveld seeing with our hands
a corporation has bored for gold and struck a seam

mineral water boils through the plate of the earth
down the pipes into this primitive rock-pool

where one day a mine and a city will be built
you can see if you must see a layer of silver steam

the thorn-trees are browsed upon by light
they take it from us not the moon

we are luminous you and I do you remember?
you reflect and I reflect like heliographs

there is phosphorus beneath our skin
like batteries we have stored the whole of life

when your hand connects with my hand
a trail of sparks scratches the dead

do you remember I said some poems
should try to talk of night-bodies?

that seeping subterranean heat unbuckled us
off dropped the old armour-plating section by section

the skull lifted off like a visor
the belt of knives and keys and the steel-edged boots fell

and now the poem extends the call-up is over
the army of our nation drops its fatigues

and the sun they've been fighting for
darkly enters into them too

furious border-boys in their local bathtubs
whole commandos skinny-dipping and defenceless

and peace takes over their heart their lungs their spines
they begin to shine with non-aggression

within this thermal radiation
only lazy horseplay and goodwill is possible

their hateful operation is turning beautiful
there are no more weapons where they've been

a truce has been embraced on the frontier
it washes even into this Sandton walled garden

and with it now come all the children of the sun
from as far as Komati and Otjiwarongo

come the burnt-out wounded dispossessed
whom we have killed and keep on killing

what's left of the hunters and herders and fishers
the last people to be mined and machine-gunned

enters at last the circle of the glare
there is no way to wall them out any more

and the first dead big-bellied child died of battling
climbs to the top of the chute poised

like a sine-curve on the dazzling light
for take-off into the sun's luxury.

CROSSING THE DESERT

This is the landscape of prophecy the ancient Namib
tilted sand from the mountains desert upon desert
from Okahandja Okazize Wilhelmstad Karibib

the N71 where the squat graves of the Mahareros assert
the honour of rebellion by a deep dry riverbed
where the municipal pool's wired in on blue alert

where towering koppies named for kaisers long dead
helmeted in ironstone clad in the yellow braid of acacia
commemorate colonial massacres and the railhead

the low of cattle now the meat-rack of Namibia
this is carcass land where blood is cheaper than rain
turning west we travel through rocks like a brazier

the tyres fry on the tar the highway leads where they came
there are crows which mean carrion bugs on the windshield
we are warned of kudu vaulting from Francoisfontein

over the foot-and-mouth fence the embankment the four-wheeled
vehicle like a capsule comfortable against the descent
down an escarpment hiding nothing all revealed

but once the marble hills fade the bushes relent
and only stones flower and the grasses thin
into the rubble of eternity piled and spent

there is Usakos corrugated white and buckled tin
and Ebony Arandis Rössing where the sky's red
Spitzkuppe to steer by on the planet's rim

at 80 kms an hour there I lifted my eyes from the dead
world into the next world saw instead of tortured lava flows
new courses geysers wells channels a fountainhead

there where we have been eroded and worn destroyed arose
exactly what mad visionaries see in the wilderness
a celestial city welcoming wide wondrous I suppose

by definition it must contain all qualities we in our viciousness
can never maintain floating as in a dream
caressed with the perfect hand of gentleness

I gather it held all knowledge all peace everything supreme
in short no armaments no sirens no hatred no police
it was the only place I knew where things were what they seem

I call upon Doris Lessing Saint John William Blake Nongqawuse
even without God they're all the same these heavenly projections
seen by prophets disgusted with the long tyranny of woes

when will this empire fall at last release subjection
when in the name of those who first challenged the status quo
did humankind first conjure this alternative perfection?

turning left a few degrees we go where we have to go
a Coke sign a palm-tree the sea-breeze rolling down mist
and in Swakopmund we find a tourist bungalow

tonight we swim in the sea drink beer get pissed
Eve they say rose from Adam's rib Christ from a herder's crib
we have crossed the desert to pink dunes foggy damp and blessed.

CHAMBER MUSIC AT MOUNT GRACE

The still sad music of humankind!
in a country of words without dialogue
a festival to celebrate this apologue:
the still sad music of humankind

a string quartet here up at Mount Grace
after tea and scones on the bushveld lawn
lets a difficult score of black notes be born
as Dryden said to subdue the savage race

yes, in the turbulent burnt Transvaal
has gathered each disciplined soloist
have come to compensate for hist-
ory down in the singing cattle and kraal

words cannot make what their true sturdy
instruments can when the tension they hold
touches the bow of hair the moment of soul –
and a box of vibrations is unburdened

we are in another far lighter land now
where a fingerpad measures each micro
of acoustic... adagio, then allegro...
the home of thresholds and yes, highbrows

elite maybe, but theirs is the mastery
an arduous lesson that has to be learnt –
come together all or burn burn –
their fire flashes out in such harmony

musicians bow formally to our clumsy applause
Great God of Music, how ordinary they are
for such a close-working group interpreter!
outside can roses still bloom against the door?

I'd forgotten the faith of being like-minded
having bad temper out and sweet sound pour
in – always let there be such hours for:
the very still music of humankind.

FADE OUT

Now Dave the truck-hire man is dying
on Friday the 13th the day won't improve
caught pants-down in his prime by
that virus they took so long to name

Dave the trucker had many more active
years of grease and six to six
the wrench and spanner Lifebuoy showers
a blue chin rusting black on schedule

now spindleshanks and Dave totters
the long haul of his mumbled days
he who could long-haul bootleg fuel
or sleeplessly butter for Bokassa

can hardly complete one video
his Kelloggs shakes over the shiny table
spoon clatters the bowl for whom
diesels throbbed in dawn concert

worse – his drive has gone from his marrow
he who willed the fleet bear congos
of corn from stashed siloes in Clocolan
to reservoirs at Blue Ribbon mills

can spend the day in day out
toilet time on delivering enough
diseased waste to poison a rat
he who managed a subcontinent

his skull is rotting his blue eyes
have flashed and recorded the still
smoking fleet of Leylands and Toyotas
in the gallery of the rest of his mind

when Dave has to change the tape
of his double-hinged ghetto-blaster
he has like a puppy to go on all fours
where he curls across the rug

for whom Cape Town to Johannesburg was eleven hours
a pitstop at Three Sisters for pleasure
Beit Bridge and Victoria Falls spare parts
of socialism for Zambian copper

and it wasn't John Rolfe that got him
but tropical AIDS the green monkey
mania that enters by the tradesman's
door without passport or prejudice

Dave the driver is down to 60 ks
whose top weight was measured in tons
a lappet-faced vulture in moult
he has become his own undertaker

who kept Checkers in sunflower oil
and Indian greens from the daybreak mart
can choke on a boiled carrot
whose cock conquered a province

dangles like a cord that pulls down
the blinds and Dave dying now
test-drives his drip gropes for the
bell and cannot clasp anything

he who so muscle-firm could
abseil on a rope off a rockface
above the city for a BP commercial
well-known as a stuntman on TV

gargles on the mushrooms of bile
that sprout from his sweet lips that
drew the soul from lovers' hips
his tongue that taught palates speech

cannot call for sister in her plastic
and his last friend or two with flowers
who now too afraid zip up
like spacemen in the evil sperm

they who unzipped on radiant beaches
down his chesthairs stroked the brine
whose hips sucked from him the gush
of his freshly smelling loins

scuff beneath the bed the rank piss
that smacks death in the nose-hairs
Dave whose tang of sweat
now smells as cold as a baptism

Dave who drank his Castle on a windsurfer
can hardly down a two-handled teacup
whose nipple behind the flap of pyjama
has spread into scars and sarcomas

Dave who gave to Cancer and Red Cross
now will give to medical research
his rotten legs his honeycombed bone
his brain tangled in his blood long since

surely his people kept in Krugersdorp
whence he emerged a print of his voice
that breathed on earlobes such
commonplace affections and codes

for now Dave's sound is mere bubbles
like guppies make in circular bowls
a mean bar-room baritone was Dave's
the guitar of his voicebox is cracked

poor Dave through tubes and pipes
scratches at a prescription pad
the Pilot nib as dithery as a fly:
MY WILL... BURN ME... DAVE...

Dave's ash from the crematorium
would infect the ravaging winds
grow seedlings into plague-trees
hermetically sealed deeper than six feet

BURN ME – that is the mandate given
while Dave's cigarette dropped on his lap
is not felt through to his human flesh
he has forgotten that fire pains

worst in all the waiting he has lost
the rides rearviews overtakes
the double-line like a hemstitch
sewing up the ripped blue miles

the N1 conveyor buckled with Dave's
Trucks for Hire the hadeda
honks of horns when at sunset
the steaming team returns to base

if his circulation's stopped up then
so are the highways of his land empty
the trunk-road of his noded spine
diverted at the first of 500 lights

the last to go is touch and none touch Dave
he who elbowed nudged or patted
faithfully in a doggy hearty scrum
has become beyond a leper in his curse

beyond the reach of any intimacy
for whom like many other bodies
the intimate gave only definition
to the long loneliness of being a man

but Dave's pulse beats a bit like your own
even if his fluid's awash in lethal junk
each drop of which would soon contaminate
leach into every droplet of your own

this very long farewell my Dave
perpetuates for us unlucky Friday
your endless twilight without cure
takes us down steps keep going down

without the sequence's end you can't die
your case and many others' is too terminal
to know if any life may be redeemed:
your road is closed this tribute done.

JOHN THE CLEANER

These are the slogans of emergency men:
    CRY FREE MANDELA the WIND bursts through
LET TAMBO BE HEARD the ROOF leaks rain
    VIVA SISULU the SKY turns blue
AMANDLA count my fingers up to TEN
    SALUTE THE FALLEN COMRADES OF GUGULETU:
These are the written sounds that cannot be spoken
A flourish on a public wall a blazing token

O John the Cleaner I can hook you with letters
    Make the great mystery of script banal
I of your ruthless elders and skilled betters
    Who cannot understand your pidgin-taal
JESUS IS KING you say and I say Break your Fetters
    A thousand ks between the castle and the kraal
You've set out to read the words OFFICE TO LET
How can I escape the prison of the alphabet?

On the koppies of the city during Sunday rest
    The prophets of the kitchen there assemble
Those are the pathways leading to a crest
    For Mount Zion a backlot where fences tumble
For banners their tunics swell across the breast
    And for crooks like shepherds their sticks atremble
Beat out a rhythm on a petrol drum
Let the dancers thunder let the spirits come

From the vantage of his mobile vertical perch
    Through the green lace of a potted palm
He notes a Christmas tree left in the lurch
    RED YELLOW WHITE it signs like a burglar alarm
A branch of pine with tinsel for a church
    A gift wrap with greetings for a psalm
The receiver of such bounty is passed out in bed
Wipe the grime from the pillow near her head

My house where we meet is a cemetery of books
      Not one records your epitaph
JOHN TSHABALALA b. in a land of spooks
      In Nineteen Sixty-Five like a bull-calf
With a roar Dr Barker's nurses in doeks
      At NQUTU slice the cord in half
And for each labour accomplished each fruit shed
There was much milk and rejoicing and bread

But my pupil can neither read nor hold a pen
      MaIlliterate they class him and his followers
He bunches up the nib for me he does J-O-H-N
      He breathes on the glass as it blurs
C-A-T spells fat cat A-M-E-N amen
      D-O-G spells teargas tanks and quirts
R99 plus GST for anyone's too dear
SUMMER SALE he wipes out till the pane is clear

For first steps we choose an old abridged edition
      Of Mofolo's Christian onslaught in *Chaka*
Already the dark phrases doom our hero to perdition
      What to me is the logic of each historic marker
Is a sermon on barbarity the convert's mission
      Makes the votive flame grow slowly darker
John relives the wrestle with Satan the Serpent
Coils up the whisper till his concentration's spent

Count my fingers to five: the begging thumb
      Index middle the fourth and little one straight
Fly away Peter fly away Paul come
      Back Peter point to John it's getting late
'Why you not touch me tonight?' 'In sum
      When you have really learned to calculate
Then I'll know from your secret algebra
How many times we can shake, *my bra*.'

How can I host you now it's June 16th?
      You have a loving wife whom you surely miss
Next comes working seventeenth and eighteenth
      Without taxis or trains no welcoming kiss
The weekend and payday is the umpteenth
      But sleep well ah my comrade till the solstice
The transport of tomorrow has already kept us warm
We hold Mandela's birthday gently in our arms.

When John the Window-Cleaner winds himself up
      Through gales and thunderstorms into the cloud
May only brightness be his ceremonial cup
      May only angels sing to him aloud
Not the sirens and the wailings where we sup
      Nor the bishops and the martyrs where we're bowed
May the rope from which he hangs always endure
The pulley and the planks be secure.

LAST TO GO

Trained near Mexico as a fruit-grower,
With a Spanish name and a You-Bet accent;

On assisted passage to Durban and from a rattling truck
He staked out a slope of bush near Nelspruit;

Purty soon with the locals inspanned:
Orchards for thorn-trees and ant-hills into pawpaws;

Caraceto he named his plot, in remembrance
Of the U. S. frontier cleared across here too;

Skin cancer got him, so with his wife and capital
He pioneered forests on the cooler escarpment;

Under Finnish pines in his long retirement
He fished with old flies the trout in others' streams;

Deaf, blind, incontinent, he sat like a stump,
Poaching by feel the fingerlings he'd put in there first;

And he'd played a wicked game of rummy;
The last of the old brigade, You-Bet.

TAKEN AS READ

The question's post-theoretical:
know the baby by its birthmarks,
prating Engels, studied Stalin
(indeed he was my first nightmare);
Saussurely Derridaed, you learnt Foucault,
but loved to wallow in Barthes,
he signified the empire of your style;
a Jung man, you held a line
through Prattfalls and the feminist,
unconscious of *Love's Body* and Marcuse;
hard to teach an ageing dog tricks:
structuring, that was it, at your post –
the great debate in triplicate –
letting the adult stand (or fall)
by all this wisdom second-hand:

strike up the banned then,
publish all your hidden heresies;
this game only converts if you master it:
all right, so – what's new, South Africa?
that's my allegiance... and yours?
mine is the perpetual sentence of syntax,
the nail in the coffin that full stops.

SEASON OF VIOLENCE

has not ended; was due to close;
termination was fully announced –
prayer-day now throughout the nations –

the air is cluttered with silent words –
can't breathe for ascending petitions;
not over yet; only begun;

a derailment at Mariannhill;
Sunday is another killer in South Africa;
take a philosophical view:

'O Lord afford me detachment
from those who want to but don't know how;
bullets through flesh fly easily'

As Archbishop Tutu said Martin Luther
King said: 'those who live an eye
for any eye end up blind people'

will not end; for ever and ever;
help out now; Amen.

LETTER

I go out to post a letter get gunned down
To purchase milk in a bottle get gunned down

Go to the festival in Fordsburg to see a film
About Langston get a bomb thrown at me

Take a taxi from Bok Street with a dozen
Others get picked off arbitrarily

Squat on the banks of Benoni
Get shack razed skull stoved

Take the Soweto train get evicted
Before New Canada by vigilantes

Clubbed by police necklaced
And ridden over by an Armscor Buffalo

I go to make my complaint at Union Building
Get mugged on the lawn left for dead

Dead me do not speak so what can I say?
This letter will have to do:

I go out to post a letter get gunned down
Get gunned down.

THE THING IS

there are no mercies left
in the shameless ruthless land

'beloved country' past crying
the white milk over dark skin is spilt

the body count rises: this month's 137
unidentified corpses to be burnt on Tuesday –

claim your dead, the dead spilt
on my rocky bosom (vide Schreiner)

at least in her day she knew who they were
at least old Paton could label each cut down

these human torches have no names:
fuel for the flames.

LIBERAL FEATURE

African Jim, passed by the British Board of Censors
for general viewing (signed Harlech),
reveals in black and white the first native –

call him Jim the Million, restless in his Swazi kraal
waves his ruralite savages off
a waggon a bus a train to the wicked city

of pulsing Jazz Maniacs
mugged by his own kind a good boss-boy takes him in
they sing about this: natural harmony

as a singing waiter in a night-club shebeen
Jim takes Dolly's heart by the arm, walks her
through gang-infested slums crooning

the caption says it all: simple people
Jim can make the blues sound happy
he neither eats drinks cries for his beloved country

show your teeth Jim (whatever your name is)
on celluloid you do survive –
show the Queen: how natural's your rhythm?

DOWN TO ZERO

Iron-fisted weather: crackdown
on outdoor gatherings curfew road-blocks

(is this the only way they know?)
the last people they trust are poets –
variable coming in from the south –

night-walks are forbidden while the trains
are ridden by red-bandanaed armies:

dispersing the people – nature's police-
man drives them home to burning shacks:
the agony is people have no place to go

gone shopping gone to church no place
to which to return in inclement weather
(there is no home for 5 million people)

(is that all they know: bring down
the thunder and guns, the tyretracks
and chains, the hail, the snow?)

poets are in *their* ghettos, too:
make shelters grow while zero is reached.

RESISTANCE

The peace march to old Mayfair
Recreation Hall is legal now

– the golden banners furl up Central
young democrats of honour

but as they assemble they're warned:
brick through the fanlight

speakers of policy evacuate
before the smaller groups

if one is picked off by a cruising Kombi
they split like shrapnel

if one is killed they bear the news
all night the right-wing stalk

the streets and alleys armed
and when their quarry's home

plant bombs that blow the
thousand plates of glass out

in the frigid air at two a.m.
(my café had its wall removed)

welcome the new South African season
to complain of armed men is treason

(Costa and Audrey scoop the sugar
up in bursting litter-bags)

CONVENTIONAL WISDOM

The lay of the land is given
Resources are naturally people

The emperor may not change his clothes
There's no sense in complaining

Iron-fisted policies quash
Thin out the pickets with poison

Shoot your antagonist in the rear
Shred the files before enquiry:

The poet shreds grammar shoots
Round corners clutches banners

Holds the pen in padded flesh
Makes this complaint: No clothes!

His only resource is in the mouths of men,
Sings at burials which change the land.

RETURNEES

on their knees touch soil
a generation lost and found

frame time again and
focus on the true subject

bring expertise and vocabulary
from another world apart

apply themselves to pulling closed
the chasm between their and our lives

the great rift will soon entomb
their and our past, level all

renegotiating exile they face
privately the force of their desertion.

PROPOSITION

In those former days to say I loved you
meant I depended on you to alter my life

this did not happen: disturbance there was
but no matter how we tried no break occurred

I must thank you for trying to change me
God knows it cost you, before you left

somehow over time that difference took place
call it molecular arrangements their own code

there was no straight trajectory I have grown
apart from what I was destined to be

now love as an active agent is gone
I find I love you all the more

without conditions or expectations without
promises even or intentions, but: firmly.

Therefore I propose we try this new bond
see this time about your deeper structure.

WELCOME

Do you understand when I say Come In
I mean all of you into my parlour

And Hold on a Sec I mean touch me
Let your fingertips take my wrist

Wait a Mo means lock your eyes on mine
But are you Sure? raise them in question

For Good to See You read Ah Blue-eyes
How're you Doing? who've you been with?

Let's Take this Another Way means
Unbutton yourself let it all hang out...

When I conclude Come Again Some Time
Believe me I mean more than I say

This is the point: phatic language
No longer clasps my situation

Without desiring touch foolish noise
Hands insert best: See Ya.

BETWEEN MEN

an intimacy that has not to do
with the exclusion of others –

the cooking and cleaning of homes,
the breakage of older relationships –

this refuge of like-minded middle age
when before the next, one career is done

this sporty drinking solidarity
an adhesion that stops the drift:

playing cards until midnight past,
jack on queen and queen on king –

jokers turn up – the suited hierarchy
works a familiar world of regular values –

this is known to be merely a game;
outside the rules are changed; your turn.

THE VENICE CONNECTION

How can I make notes about your much written-over
city? co-opted in my language by Byron through James –

once through the lanes of the old Venetian Republic
you said No one has babies; we're growing old, dying –

part of my Grand Tour and late education I have had advantage
of your walk-in history, your prosecco, your unforgivable
      colours –

and much of my heart has remained in your generous flat
round the clock-tower through stalls off Saint Mark's Square,
      heavens!

hearing your voice on the phone is always a return
yet again, how intimately I know your blunt inflections, your
      tone –

nothing of our life here is Venetian: no past that isn't suppressed,
no water to make us kin, no procession from the ghetto to the
      tombs –

the palimpsest to peel back from the blueprint is missing,
here everyone's young and knows less and less –

I would take as my heritage your days of slavery, too,
and if I could paint, paint crowdedly down to the household dog –

inclusive panoramas and yes if you want, God Himself on high,
although on that score I remain as deeply disbelieving as you –

they've a Bridge of Sighs here from one concrete bunker
to the next where prisoners march, but that is the only
      connection –

old merchant, my friend, only this in reply to your tongue:
my greetings, my love always, teach me your staying-power.

Charles Baudelaire

TO A CREOLE

But you lady if you were to voyage with me
would conquer the old world of decay by storm
there is no way those stiff madams could ever be
equal to you in content and outward form

once I've seen your eyes open toward the veranda
and your fuzzy head beckon over your arm
once I've seen your every magical splendour
and touched my fingers on your well-oiled palm

I understand why cyclones hush around you
why roofs batten down as pale lovers sue
and the warm pressure inside turns me over too

for there is no body other than yours
no neck no skin no rind of dress on other whores
that knows why I thunder and come true.

BLACK VENUS

Don't leave your estate for a sailor's arms
don't yearn so for a passage of oceans
over there they'll flatten your unknown charms
beat you up scrape you with false potions

your innocent habitat you must preserve
even if barefoot sweeping the mats you know
the master's the one you were born to serve
and you know when he calls for you you go

for when I observe your lassitude
your delicate tread your fresh negritude
when you unshell your skirt and step nude

into the water tank and fish nudge a kiss
on your nipples and roll on in a warm bliss
I know no part of you was made for servitude.

THE ALBATROSS

Becalmed out of their depth on a bored swell
the sails wrung out and stiff as their shirts
the creak of the rigging and the foggy bell
their chant low from where it hurts

they lassoed in an albatross poor guard
of our night crossing planer of air
on deck like a stricken lopsided bard
his wings like oars beyond all repair

and some poked with a pipe-stem at his eye
some stroked his yellow bill and asked why
he looked so fallen did he miss his sky

and such railing laughter each time he lifted
a streamlined foot and slewed over and shifted
down the hatch and could no longer fly.

SAILING HOME

O Atlantic breakers throttled with seaweed
I ride you on a proud hull from safe
land to the limits of man's passionate need
levelling your storms to the outermost wave

o turbulence there is more contained
within my churn of opium and Nuit St George
that the furthest ripple constrained
by the coast or the walls of my gorge

o implacable enemy take my might
take my learning take the sight
of a bold venturer astride the deck and fight

your discontent can never outlast mine
take my spit for all your raging brine
o blue wrestler o moon-soft night.

Anon.

THE CONCERT

*A Griqua describes in the Taal the first concert held in the
schoolroom, Kokstad, 1876*

A concert's what the English like,
    Their best clothes they put on;
Never mind if it's day or night,
    They're always game to have some fun.

With wife and child that's where he'll trot,
    For talk and laughing and to sing;
They like their kind of sport a lot,
    It goes on and on without ending.

So I was very keen to see
    What type of show makes them swarm;
That they can spend such good money
    To hear a Rooinek perform.

With a swallow-tail a big black coat
    I borrowed from Brother Sem,
From Uncle Gert a shilling, a shirt –
    Then I was just like them.

Now in I go with a proud tread,
    I sit on the foremost bench,
Of the local whites I am never scared,
    So what do I owe to them?

The house was full. Ah, it was grand
    To see such happy settlers here;
Gents and girls sit hand in hand.
    All I lacked was an interpreter.

They played and sang with wild applause,
    Each minute something fresh and fit;
They improvised with never a pause –
    Not that I grasped a word of it!

Then came an item that I confess
    Put me in great apprehension
Ten black fellows in fancy dress
    Each with a kind of violin

Entered and lolled upon a stool,
    Their hair frizzed out in great display,
Rowdy and ugly and each a fool –
    I shivered on the spot, I say.

I thought to myself, what's going to be
    From where are they appearing?
Are they Negro folk from oversea,
    Or are those masks they're wearing?

Well, masks they certainly were not;
    It was bootblack on their skin;
Where one had wiped his lips all hot
    I saw the jaw of Sergeant Glynn.

So they dance and play the stupid coon,
    Ten creatures on a spree;
When all at once I almost swoon –
    They point and wink at me:

The brown man! Oh, in my own hall,
    To be the object of their laughter!
In all the noise my bitter gall
    Was going to boil for ever after!

We laboured hard to build this school
    Where all our children can learn;
Now there seems they've made a rule
    To drive us from our home again.

Well, blood is thicker that water once more,
    For darkies as well as for fair,
If you scratch too much an open sore
    The pain is hard to bear.

So 'Christy Minstrels' is what they're called;
    Don't they have any shame? –
To give such a really godless act
    Such a very lovely name?

Eugène N. Marais

RADIO CRADLE SONG

Sleep, little Baby, kip in peace through the night,
Little Angels often guard you in your plight.
Sleep calmly to the hymns of Radio J. B.:
'I want to be happy' and 'Take me to tea'.

Your pa's playing bridge and your ma tries the same,
And it's Ayah's apostolic birthday yet again,
But for you, sweet Babe, the radio steams on:
'Bananas' and 'Show me the way to go home'.

When Mummy and Daddy were still little brats,
They had no choice between Foxtrots and Jazz,
Never your privileges, my Darling, had they:
'Me and the Boy Friend' and 'Just for the day'.

Sleep sweetly, Little Pixie, sweetly through the night,
Your little lips laugh, but your eyes are held tight;
Your Daddy is a prowler and Mum the kiss of death,
But the programme is J. B., so Happy New Year.

Jean-Joseph Rabearivelo

TALL TREES

I have not come to pillage the fruits
that you hold out, on your unreachable crests,
to the people of the stars and the tribe of the winds,
nor to tear down the flowers I have never seen before,
meaning to wear them or hide some shame I overlook,
I who am a child of barren hills.

But it suddenly came to me in my last sleep
that always I was tethered in the lianas of the night
like the old pirogue of fables
in which all the days of my youth were passed,
from the shores of evening to the shores of dawn,
from the cape of the moon to the cape of the sun.

I've hauled myself out, and here at your heart I am,
    mountain of plants!
Here I have come to question your absolute silence,
to seek for the place where the winds are hatched
before they reach us, their wings full of holes,
broken by the immense net of the deserts
and by the snares of inhabited towns.

What do I hear and see, tallest of trees?
Here are lost sounds to recover which are lost again,
like underground rivers
crossed by enormous blind birds
carried off by the rapid currents
to be engulfed in slime.

It's your breath, your breath so deep
and already as sore as an old man's
climbing the coast of his memories
descending the slope of his exhausted days.
Your breath, and the breath of innumerable birds,
and of your branches grazed by the whole apocalyptic world.

But what may I see in your colourless night,
your night lasting longer that the death of virtuous men,
and the life of the wretched poor,

cave of leaves, out of which maybe one passage leads to the shore
and another to the horizon's hell,
you like a rainbow binding the continents?

I see nothing but the sun sinking,
like a pig assegaied in the scrub of the sky,
pig of light taken in powerful nets
that you spring in your ripe fruit and tough flowers,
high up, down there, at the extreme limit
where the spirit of earth and the force of the tree meet.

But later, even though the days are numberless
as your succession of leaves already fallen to hell,
even though the sevenfold nights have thickened
the night of time more than seven times,
so that I may gather the flowering dawns
at the end of the broken stalks of dusk,
I will always keep the memory of your silence
and of your strange clarity.

They'll be like pebbles thrown on the sand,
collected by an old sailor
who carries them home, placing them besides the shell
of a balanced miniature pirogue
bought in a distant isle that only a dream inhabits,
but where huts line the sea.

Rather they'll be like unworked pieces of ebony,
of rosewood or some other precious stuff
that I will place on my table
where your memory will slowly carve them
into fetishes with glassy eyes,
silent fetishes between my books.